TWENTY IDEAS FOR 2020

By
Patrick Barber, Ph.D.

Table of Contents

20 IDEAS
for
VOTE
2020

Introduction

The election in the United States in November 2020 will be an extremely important one. It should focus on principles rather than party politics. The determining factor for the election must be which candidates will serve the nation best rather than which political party will win. If the election is decided by politics rather than principles, the nation loses.

For principles to take centerstage in the 2020 election, ideas must be presented and discussed by the electorate. The current emphasis on personalities and parties must be replaced by discussions and debates over creative ideas to address the nation's many needs and problems. In these pages the reader will find twenty ideas which are put forward as suggestions to be considered. The author hopes that readers find the suggestions given in these pages stimulate new and perhaps better ideas to be formulated and put forward. In the end, the goal is for America to move forward to a brighter future characterized by intelligence, compassion, and competence. It must abandon lies, bullying, ignorance, and incompetence.

1. Field a Complete Slate in 2020

The United States of America does not at the present time have a President. It does have a <u>C</u>urrent <u>T</u>emporary <u>W</u>hite House <u>O</u>ffice <u>O</u>ccupant [C TWO O or C_2O].[1] Real Presidents unite the diverse electorate of the nation behind a vision of the future. He or she does not ask the nation to take a nostalgic walk back into the past where the nation was the leader of the free world and was the world's greatest economy. Rather real Presidents have visions that look forward. It may have been a call to "Make the World Safe for Democracy" [Woodrow Wilson], or "The only thing you need to fear is fear itself" [FDR], or "Land a Man on the Moon and Bring Him Home Safely by the End of the Decade" [JFK]. With this American leadership, three European Empires were overthrown at the end of World War I, the horror of the Holocaust and the terror of Nazism were terminated at the end of World War II, and American men did land on the moon and return safely before the end of the 1960's. Yes, all these were done with American women participating actively!

These heroic actions in the past always paved the way to a brighter future not only for Americans but also for the world. New nations were created at the ends of the two World Wars. Peoples in Europe and the Middle East were freed from the confines of empires at the end of World War I, and peoples of Africa and Asia developed

---

[1] If the reader really dislikes the present C_2O, he could be called "C_2O-ah-oh."

new nations from old empires after World War II. A new economic order for the world was also developed with American leadership after the 1944 Breton Woods meeting. This led to better prosperity and economic stability for many nations. America led the way with a vision that was tempered by lessons learned from painful wars and the Great Depression. America led with real Presidents who put forward ideas that united the nation and moved the world.

The present C_2O provides no vision of a better future, he has presented no new ideas, he has failed to unite all Americans behind his non-existent vision, and he only seems interested in protecting his own personal and financial interests. He is good at placing blame on others and claiming all credit for himself. No. Such has never been the actions and words of a real American President.

One of the foremost abilities of a real American President is the ability to find, vet, hire, and retain the most talented citizens to serve in his or her cabinet, on the White House executive staff, and to completely fill vacant positions in the executive branch. The present C_2O has demonstrated repeatedly over several years that he cannot do this basic task of the Office of President. He may have won an election, but he has abandoned the presidency.

Such a failure affords those who seek to replace him with an opportunity. The Democratic Party in 2019 held a series of public debates among many declared presidential candidates. Not all of them can become President, but they all showed great skills, talents, and dedication to service.   At least one political party in America may be willing to serve rather than to be served.

Those who plan to win in November 2020 should present to the American electorate more than just presidential and vice-presidential candidates. The winning party should also prepare a full slate of talented individuals for all cabinet secretaries and many important executive offices.   The existing C_2O obviously will be unable to match such an accomplishment, for in three years since his election he has still not filled all vacancies and kept them filled with competent individuals. When the new President takes office in January 2021 with a full slate of cabinet and executive office nominees, the executive branch will be fully staffed and ready to get down to work. They will need an early start to make up all the ground lost under the C_2O.

A new Congress begins early in January 2021. It will have about three weeks to interview the executive office nominees and may be able to or at least get ready to give Senate approval to them. These executive officers will then be able to begin work immediately after Inauguration Day later in January.

Who should be the Presidential nominee? The answer is obvious. The man or woman who has the vision and leadership skills to persuade other talented American candidates and individuals to join this winning team should be the presidential nominee.

2. **Gun Control**

When the Second Amendment to the U.S. Constitution was written and adopted at the end of the eighteenth century, the only firearms that existed were single-shot, muzzle loaded ones. A well-trained marksman could load and fire up to three rounds a minute. No one even imagined that a weapon could be loaded from the breach. No one had any idea of how such a weapon could be made to work safely and reliably. This Second Amendment applied and still applies today only to single-shot weapons. If this constitutional guarantee is to be extrapolated to include multi-shot weapons that came into existence more than a century after the adoption of the Bill of Rights, then there needs to be a new amendment written, passed, and adopted to cover these innovations. Until such an amendment is adopted, the Second Amendment must not be extrapolated to include modern, multi-shot weapons. One must not read into the Constitution something that is not there and in fact was never imagined at the time of adoption.

Some may not see the fallacy of blindly extrapolating an eighteenth-century document to the twenty-first century situation. To help such individuals see the error of their thinking, imagine that the Second Amendment to the Constitution also had an additional clause giving Americans the "right to own and operate wheeled vehicles without interference." Imagine the situation that would exist on America's highways if such an additional clause were extrapolated to include modern automobiles and trucks rather than just horse-drawn carts. It would not be possible to impose speed limits, to require seat belts and airbags, or to install and enforce yield signs, stop signs, or traffic lights. Texting-while-driving would still be stupid, but it could not be regulated or forbidden. Automotive insurance could not be required. DUI could not be a crime. One-way streets would not exist! Imagine that the AAA adopted the fight-it-at-all-cost attitude that the NRA has taken with guns! Who among us would want to drive or let our loved ones use a roadway? Instead there is no such imaginary additional clause, and the AAA is one of strongest advocates for automotive safety. No. The Second Amendment to the Constitution applies only to single-shot firearms until such time as an additional amendment is adopted to expand those rights to modern, multi-shot weapons having magazines.

If the United States had a real President, he or she could take immediate executive action to begin reigning in gun violence in the nation. A simple executive order could deny all federal highway funds to any state that did not forbid operational, multi-shot firearms from being present together with ammunition on a public roadway. These weapons, if taken on a roadway, must be securely locked with a trigger lock or other such device. They must not be loaded. For a first violation of that regulation, the firearm and any and all ammunition found to be or have been on a public roadway in an operational fashion must be confiscated without compensation. For a second offense, all multi-shot weapons and ammunition in the possession of or in the residence or workplace of the offender must be confiscated without compensation. A person with two such convictions will be forbidden from owning or having access to firearms.

Harsh? Hardly. In Virginia it is already against the hunting regulations for anyone to discharge a weapon, single- or multi-shot, within 100 yards of a highway or within 300 yards of an occupied dwelling. There simply is no reason for anyone to have a multi-shot weapon together with its ammunition in an operational state on or adjacent to a public roadway. Multi-shot firearms may be transported on or near public highways only if securely locked and unloaded.

The gun violence that exists today in America has created victims, who are due compensation. Any and all sales of ammunition should carry a surcharge to contribute to a fund used to compensate victims of gun violence. The level of violence will determine the size of the surcharge. If gun owners want to reduce the cost of their ammunition, they must work actively to promote sane and safe gun ownership. The NRA must adopt proactive safety policies analogous to those adopted by the AAA for highway safety.

The writers of the Bill of Rights were correct when they observed that a well trained and equipped militia serves to protect the nation against external aggressors. The federal government should work with the National Guard in each state to establish a series of federally licensed firing ranges. These ranges will teach and promote the safe handling of weapons, their proper maintenance, and the proficient use of each owner's guns.

Any citizen who demonstrates proficiency, safe handling, and marksmanship will be recognized as a national marksman. National marksmen[2] may be exempt from monthly fees to use the firing ranges if they volunteer to teach gun safety, firearm maintenance, and marksmanship at licensed ranges. Establish a reasonably high standard to become recognized as a marksman. Any aggressor will have to think twice or more before invading a country in which 50 million citizens are armed with weapons that they can use to hit 1-foot diameter targets 92% of the time at 100 yards.

---

[2] This collective noun as well as others in this book include both males and females. There are female marksmen. There are no female marks or markspersons.

3. Healthcare

Affordable healthcare should and must be available to all U.S. citizens and residents, but no one individual, insurance company, or lawyer should be able to abuse the system to become rich. It must be available to all but must not be a gift to either the rich or poor.

In order to make this possible for all, regardless of income, the task should be divided into three parts. If it is free and available to all, it will be subject to abuse and overuse by a few. If there were a set minimum fee to be paid up front by all, the system would be unfair to the poor. To mitigate this dilemma, make the first level payable by all; but make the amount to be paid dependent upon the patient's income. As an example of how the system could work, first compute a person's or family's three-year average adjusted gross income, <3yrAGI>. Use ten percent of this figure as the maximum amount each patient or family must pay up front each year for healthcare services. To help ease the burden of such payments, each person or family could contribute to an individual, tax-sheltered healthcare fund from which such payments could be taken.

Above this initial threshold, private health insurance could be purchased. The only factor to be considered when establishing the cost of such health insurance would be the age at which the patient begins and continues to purchase such insurance. Pre-existing conditions could not be considered. The sooner a person or family begins participation in healthcare insurance the lower will be their annual premiums. If they wait years to begin participating, their annual premiums will be higher. If a patient cannot find an affordable private insurance policy, the state or federal government will make one or more plans available. These policies could be private or public ones. Private insurance companies must compete to provide a better service at a lower cost than available from the government. These companies are creative and can meet that challenge so that all Americans will benefit. The healthcare system in America can be something of which the nation can be proud and something copied by other nations. Affordable health insurance must be available to all but not required.

All private health insurance policies must be portable among the states. Clients must not be restricted as to where they can live and work because of the availability of health insurance. Employers may wish to help pay for employee health insurance as a benefit of employment, but they may not use such health insurance coverage to prevent or discourage employees from changing jobs.

These private health insurance policies have a lower limit of coverage, e.g., 10% <3yrAGI>. They also should have an upper limit of say 10 times <3yrAGI>. Above this upper limit, private health insurance is not needed and should not be available. Above this upper limit, the federal government will cover healthcare costs possibly under an extension of Medicare. No person should be forced into bankruptcy because of catastrophic disease, and no insurance company should be able to use the possibility of extremely high medical costs for a few to increase costs for everyone.

Consider as an example the family whose <3yrAGI> is $50,000. Their out of pocket healthcare expenses each year will be a maximum of $5,000. They or their employer may purchase private or public health insurance for medical expenses above that amount up to a maximum of $500,000. The federal government, under an extension of the existing Medicare program, will cover expenses above this maximum insurance limit.

The poor earning less than either the full-time minimum wage for 2080 hours per year or the accepted poverty level will have to have a charity program to help cover their out-of-pocket medical and health insurance expenses. During the initial enrollment under the new program, provision will also have to be made for those who are now able to join but who are already old. These enrollees cannot be penalized the same as someone who could have enrolled at eighteen years of age but who waited until reaching sixty to purchase health insurance. The Medicare program for residents over 65 years of age would continue. The private Medicare supplement insurance program could continue as currently exists. There no longer would be a need for a Medicaid program unless that becomes the program under which the poor have access to health care and insurance.

To keep medical costs down to a reasonable amount, state and federal governments should establish norms for charges that can be levied. A table of ordinary, reasonable, and allowable charges for medical procedures and pharmaceuticals should be established and enforced. If doctors, hospitals, clinics, or pharmacies wish to charge more than allowed, they must be required to provide reasons why individual cases are more expensive than normal. Permission must be obtained before exceeding the allowed charges. Charging $110.00 to administer an aspirin tablet will no longer be allowed. Charging different amounts for the same basic procedure will no longer be tolerated. Charging insured patients an amount different from the uninsured will no longer be permitted.

There may be a social benefit, however, in permitting health insurance companies to charge higher premiums to individuals who voluntarily, for their own pleasure or benefit, choose to engage in hazardous activities. Such activities as driving while intoxicated or under the influence of illegal drugs or driving while texting would be examples of such hazardous activities that if discouraged would reduce everyone's health care costs and benefit the individual as well as the nation.

Everyone would also benefit if all health insurance policies encouraged periodic medical examinations at no out-of-pocket expense to the patient. Every person not under treatment who is younger than 18 or over 60 years of age should be able to have one checkup each year. Every person not under treatment between those ages should be able to have one checkup every five years. Catching and treating diseases early is both cost effective and allows for more successful treatments.

It would also help to keep health care costs down if lawyers were kept out of medical decisions and if pharmaceutical companies were rewarded for keeping prescription drug costs down. Refer to the next two topics.

4. **Pharmaceutical Reform**

To provide all Americans access to healthcare, without providing limits on healthcare costs, will not solve the nation's healthcare crisis. An obvious place to begin is with a general principle – no person or company should get rich from another person's misfortune. Companies that provide healthcare are due a reasonable but limited return on their investment. It must never be a route to exorbitant riches at someone else's expense.

Reforming the pharmaceutical industry is one place to begin. Doing so without reducing creativity is the challenge. There are several factors that cause the inflation of pharmaceutical costs. One is the excessive amount of advertising done by the industry to the public. Members of the general public are generally not trained enough in science and medicine to be able to judge the efficacy and validity of advertised claims. The general public is the wrong audience to which to present medical claims. No advertising costs to the public for pharmaceuticals should be counted as a cost of development or of doing business. When a company develops a greatly improved drug, a simple printed or electronic flyer sent only to licensed medical practitioners should be enough. That audience is capable of understanding and evaluating the claims and evidence. Why waste the public's time and money unless the company wishes to push a new drug off on an unsuspecting but hopeful public?

Second, an excessive wages rule should be rigorously enforced. Any wage or benefit paid to any

16

employee or consultant in excess of the wage for the President of the United States, i.e., $400,000 currently, should not be counted as a business expense. Any amount over that limit must count as company profits and taxes must be paid.[3]

Third, the major cost of developing a new drug for market is the extensive testing required. American pharmaceutical companies should be able to participate in a government development program that requires drug companies to complete only the first level of testing at their expense. They must prove that the new drug is not harmful or toxic. The next two levels of testing which show that the drug is effective and that it is better than already existing ones will be done in Federal laboratories, supervised or licensed by the FDA and paid for by the federal government. In exchange, the drug companies agree to price the new drug in the U.S. at actual development costs. No excessive wages, benefits, or advertising costs will be counted in the calculation. A modest, e.g., 5%, profit would be allowed. This would be an example of government-private industry partnership. This is not socialism.

Companies not taking advantage of this program will still be subjected to some limits on what they can

---

[3] An alternative way to limit company costs would be to use a different upper limit. Rather than the salary of the President, a fixed multiple of the lowest salary paid by a company to any of its employees or full-time contractors could be used. For example, the upper limit for counting as a business expense could be 12 to 17 times the lowest salary in the company.

charge, but they may find a little more flexibility. They will not be able to charge whatever they can squeeze out of the public, patients, or health insurance companies. Pharmaceutical companies may only advertise to licensed medical professionals. They may not advertise to the general public in print, electronic media, radio, television, or the U.S. mail. Incentives and bonuses or perks may not be paid to medical professionals to increase sales.

5. **Limit the Legal Profession's Reach into Medical Care**

The costs to protect medical professionals from lawsuits adds unnecessarily to the costs of delivering quality medical care. Often it is only lawyers who bank the bulk of any settlements. Society should place barriers to retard the legal profession's foray into medicine. Before a medical malpractice lawsuit can be considered by a court of law, the following must be completed in a timely manner.

Each potential case must first be reviewed by a civilian medical review board appointed by state governors for each health district in each state. The members appointed to the local review boards must be knowledgeable, intelligent, honorable men and women resident in the health district. They may not be lawyers and the majority may not be medical professionals. Lawyers and additional medical professionals may be hired as consultants to these boards. Members of these local boards may receive up to the federally allowed per diem reimbursement and may also receive only a small honorarium. The local boards will have up to thirty days to consider each case, hear testimony, review evidence, and render a decision as to whether medical malpractice or fraud had been committed.

Each case will automatically be reviewed by the state medical examiner after the local review board has rendered its decision. The examiner must also render a decision in no more than thirty additional days.

Only after the state medical director rules on a case may lawyers become involved and proceed as is now the situation. The entire administrative review process must be expeditious, being completed in thirty to sixty days or less. Lawyers will be discouraged from chasing ambulances and will have a much higher standard to reach before claiming medical malpractice.

6. Prison Reform

The current reliance on incarceration to rehabilitate criminals is a failure. Prisons and jails are merely graduate schools for felons. Society would benefit more if criminals were afforded opportunities to better themselves and were held responsible for doing so. It is time to place the burden of reform back onto the felons themselves. Provide them with a choice that enables them, if they rise to meet the challenge, to re-enter society as productive contributors rather than takers.

When a person commits and is convicted of committing a crime, have the state compensate both the victims and insurance companies. The convicted criminal then is given a choice. He or she may elect to be incarcerated as now is done. Alternatively, he or she may elect to become an indentured servant to the state until the debt, which the state paid out, has been paid back to the state. He or she must pay the state back this debt by obtaining and maintaining a job and making regular payments on his or her debt. The state should help the felon secure a first job by offering opportunities to master skills needed to secure a job or a better one. A set, agreed-upon percentage of each paycheck will be sent to the state to discharge the debt incurred by the criminal. When the debt is paid back, the felon is free. If the convict participating in the program holds a job, makes regular reimbursement payments to the state, and commits no additional crimes, the convict may live and work in society. His location must be monitored; but other than that, it is expected that it is his or her responsibility to be a productive and contributing member of society bettering himself or herself while he discharges the debt to the state.

Because the rich must not be able to escape justice by quickly paying back their debt to the state from high-valued assets or high salaries, all reimbursements to the state must come from current salary. Any such prisoner who obtains and holds a job paying more than twice the minimum wage may use only funds earned from that job up to twice minimum wage. All salary amounts in excess of this are to be held in trust by the state to be returned to the prisoner upon completion of repayment. The state shall also hold all property and assets of the felon in trust until the debt has been repaid from funds earned from a current job. If the felon is married or has assets held jointly, an equitable division of these shall be made at the beginning of the repayment program.

Any prisoner participant who commits a subsequent crime while on this work-release program will forfeit all property and proceeds held in trust by the state. While funds and assets are being held in trust by the state, the state will collect any interest and proceeds earned by the trust and use these to fund the program. Only the property and the principal shall be returned to the felon upon discharge of his debt.

The felon will be empowered to modify the length of his sentence by his future actions. If he elects to live frugally and use a large percentage of his income to discharge his debt, he may be released early. If he successfully completes training and obtains a better job, he may pay down his debt more quickly and shorten his sentence by half. While in a training program he will be paid at least the state minimum wage.

On the other hand, if he fails to secure and retain a job and to make regular payments, he will lengthen his sentence. If he commits another felony while under this program, he loses this option and must be incarcerated until the debt is discharged. While incarcerated, the cost of his incarceration shall be added to his debt and he loses all that has been held in trust for him. While incarcerated he will be given the opportunity to work for at least the minimum wage. If he obtains additional skills to be able to be employed at a higher rate while incarcerated, he could still find ways to shorten his period of incarceration. Failing to work positively will only lengthen his time in prison and delay his release back into society.

Felons committing violent crimes with lethal weapons and those who present a clear and present danger to others do not have a choice. They must complete their sentence and pay their debt while incarcerated.

The state has some obligations under this program. It must make education and training opportunities available to enrollees. It can encourage but not force participation in programs to improve the prisoner's employability. It must help the felon secure at least a first job and educate him about skills and personality traits that will help him hold that job and obtain promotions.

Convicted criminals participating in the work-release program must take the initiative to obtain and retain a job and to make regular repayments. Sentences will be modified by each prisoner's actions and attitudes. He or she can, by actions and attitude, shorten or lengthen their sentences and can determine the size of the trust that is received upon release. With care, a criminal could regain freedom with job skills and a bank account.

7. **Income Disparity**

An American working full-time for 2080 hours per year at a minimum wage of $10/hour will earn about $20,800 in a year. He will take home and must support himself and family on that amount less federal and state income taxes, social security taxes, Medicare and Medicaid taxes, health insurance fees, sales taxes, gasoline taxes, Trump Tariff Taxes (T^3 taxes), etc. He will indeed be fortunate if he has half of what he earned to support himself and his family. Can an American today really buy food, housing, transportation, clothing, and other necessities for life on less than $1000/month? Will he have enough left for his children to buy a stick of chewing gum?

On the other side of the coin there are Americans who make in one quarter what the previous example made in an entire year. This American realizes an annual salary of $83,200. Some even make in one month what the minimum wage earner makes in a year, i.e., $249,600. What about those in the high earner categories who make in a week, a day, or an hour what others struggle to make in an entire year? Are there even some who make the minimum annual income in a minute? The table below shows the annual salaries for workers who earn in a given shorter period what a minimum wage earner makes in an entire year.

		SALARY TABLE
The Basic Salary =	$	20,800
This Basic Amount Earned in		
one year	$	20,800
one quarter	$	83,200
one month	$	249,600
one week	$	1,081,600
one day	$	7,592,000
one hour	$	182,208,000
one minute	$	10,932,480,000
one second		$655,948,800,000

Such a situation is blatantly unfair. If the economic system refuses to level this out, the government must do so for the sake of social order and fairness. It must be careful, however, that in doing so it does not remove or reduce the incentives for creativity and hard work.

Such is the error of Socialism and Communism that I observed while visiting and living briefly in the GDR (East Germany) on the other side of the Iron Curtain in the 1980's and 1990's. Socialism fails to find ways to encourage and reward hard work and creativity. It tries to compel these and fails to do so. Awarding an Ehrenpfannen (a banner of honor from the GDR homeland) just does not motivate as much as a promotion or a bonus in a paycheck. These virtues must be stimulated from within individuals and not compelled from outside. Fear will not be effective either. The NAZI Holocaust and the Chinese Great Leap Forward proved that fact. The STAZI of East Germany were unable to motivate the people of the GDR. They tried using fear and greed. The people simply replied (silently), "You pretend to pay us, and we pretend to work." No. To be successful, motivation must arise from within each citizen. Society's challenge is to find ways to stimulate, motivate, and reward such socially beneficial behavior. In America's capitalistic system, this has been done successfully by relying on families, education, and opportunity. It worked. Just look around you. Try to find a successful Socialist system. Zimbabwe destroyed a successful capitalist economy and became an importer rather than an exporter of food. Chairman Mao almost obliterated China during the Cultural Revolution. The Ehrenpfannen of East Germany are only displayed in museums today.

So now what? Socialism fails. Communism has even been abandoned by its most ardent advocates. Capitalism as it exists today is clearly unfair and headed for social chaos. The simplest, but perhaps not the only, solution is to have a tax system that is fair so that those who have benefitted from the economic system most, return the most.

Those who work for minimum wage should be expected to pay a minimum in taxes, but they must still pay something. For example, those attempting to live on a minimum wage salary might pay no more than $5.00/month in federal and state income taxes. Those who make in a month what other make in a year should pay more. This should go up steeply as the time required to earn a minimum salary becomes shorter. Return, perhaps, to the time when high income earners paid 75% or more in income taxes.

Because it is desirable to encourage high income earners and corporations to do more to benefit others, create a bracket in which a tax payer could keep a larger portion of the excessive income if he or she could prove with employer ID numbers and W-2's that this excessive income was used to create jobs for others.

To also help dampen this unhealthy drive for obscene incomes, put two further limits in place. Any organization that claims to be non-profit must not pay anyone more than the President of the U.S. is paid. Doing so should render that organization a for-profit one.

Any company may pay their officers whatever they wish. Any compensation in wages or benefits that exceeds the current annual salary of the U.S. President, i.e., $400,000/year, may no longer count as a business expense. These excessive wages and benefits must be counted as profit and corporate taxes paid on them.[4]

---

[4] See also the alternative limit under Idea 4, Pharmaceutical Reform.

8. Climate Change and Global Warming

The scientific data on climate change is almost overwhelming and is denied only by those who continue to shut their eyes to what is happening around them. There are recorded temperature data going back a century or more that show the atmospheric temperature has increased, glaciers have retreated all over the globe, the polar ice caps are disappearing, and the ocean depth has increased. In addition to this data, one of my colleagues at Longwood University, Professor Alton Harvill, his wife, and several volunteer botanists worked throughout the Commonwealth of Virginia for almost a half century. Since Virginia is situated mid-way up the Atlantic seaboard of North America, one can learn about climate changes from recording how plants move across the state.   This dedicated group gathered, dried, identified, catalogued, and documented the locations of plants in Virginia for almost a half-century. Dr. Harvill prepared several editions of his plants of Virginia over this time and showed that southern plants were moving north through the state. This herbarium collection is preserved at Longwood University in Farmville, Virginia, as the Stevens-Harvill Herbarium. Such plant migration is consistent with other data supporting global warming.

On a less rigorous but more personal basis, when I moved to Virginia in 1971 after earning a Ph.D. degree from Cornell University in upstate New York, my wife and I could ice skate on local Virginia farm ponds a couple of times each winter. I do not set foot on such ice unless it is several inches thick. We have not found that we could do this in decades.

Global warming is a fact of 21st Century life on Earth. It may not be so clearly demonstrated that this was caused only by human activity generating greenhouse gases. The earth's temperature has fluctuated repeatedly throughout geological time alternating between ice ages and warming periods. Whether or not humans cause global warming is irrelevant.

The opportunities afforded by developing alternative sources of energy to replace fossil fuels are great and are beckoning. Solar, wind, advanced (i.e., post-1950's) nuclear, tidal, geothermal, and yet to be imagined sources promise a wonderful future with abundant energy and a clean environment. Let's all get busy!

I understand smog and pollution, and I do not want to return to having to live in it. I lived in Southern California in the 1950's and 1960's. When I looked west from the San Bernardino Mountains toward the Pacific Ocean, all I could see poking above the blanket of smog were the two peaks of Saddleback Mountain, the highest points in Orange County. I wondered how anyone would want to live in that. Then I realized that I too would have to return to that polluted atmosphere when my summer job ended.

Going back to relying on coal, petroleum, and natural gas retards the development of new and cleaner sources of energy. While other nations surge ahead, America remains stuck fast to dangerous, archaic technologies originally developed in the nineteenth century at the start of the Industrial Revolution. It is as if America were Brer Fox with his fists stuck fast in the Tar Baby. We should be more creative like Brer Rabbit and hop enthusiastically into the future.

9. **Economic Opportunities for Growth**

When one steps back and honestly looks at what made America great, one obtains a clearer idea of what it will take to keep this greatness going in the future. To say "Make America Great Again" is a clear admission that your vision is focused only on the past rather than the future.

Look at some specific historical illustrations of political actions that greatly improved America. Three industries making large positive contributions to America's economy and its balance of payments today are agriculture, aviation, and electronics. How did this come about?

Yes, it helps that America is blessed with abundant arable land and water and has beneficial weather. A smart, forward looking government was also required. In the depths of the American Civil War, the U.S. Government passed the Merrill Act that established a series of Land Grant Colleges and Universities. One mission of these institutions was to work with and for farmers to increase agricultural productivity. This worked. Farmers in America became better educated and new knowledge was developed and disseminated enabling America's farms to produce more at less cost. It also helped that America stimulated and rewarded creativity resulting in a new plough that enabled the thick soil of the Great Plains to be turned over and resulting in the McCormick reaper that reduced the time and labor involved in harvesting some crops. With help from the state agricultural institutions and agents, American farmers gained access to the latest and best technologies, seeds, fertilizers, chemicals, and agricultural practices. After World War I, it was America that fed the world.

The Wright Brothers of Ohio were able to move from repairing bicycles to inventing airplanes because the American government in their day actually answered letters of inquiry from citizens in a timely manner. The U.S. Weather Service did answer the Wright Brother's letter inquiring about a suitable location to test their new flying machine. The government reply suggested Kitty Hawk, North Carolina, as a location that had the necessary wind speeds.

After the first successful heavier than air flights, the U.S. Government continued to support the developing field of aviation. In 1917 it established Langley Field in Hampton, Virginia, as a government test facility with large, expensive wind tunnels and other testing facilities to aid the further development of aviation. Private industries were encouraged to avail themselves of these federal facilities. The result was the emergence of aircraft companies such as Lockheed, Boeing, Martin-Marietta, Curtis, etc. These companies made great advances and built the fighters and bombers that helped win World War II. These government test facilities helped in the development of passenger aircraft that spanned the continents and crossed the oceans. These same facilities helped put an American on the moon.

The program to put a man on the moon was a government one, but it spurred developments that made modern computers and communication possible. The electronics age we all enjoy today is a result of this government-private industry cooperation.

Similar government-private industry cooperation and synergy will go a long way to make America Great Again in the Future. Opportunities abound in renewable energy, medicine/healthcare, genetics, nutrition, agriculture, electronics, and communications among others yet to be imagined. This is not socialism. It is government stimulating and supporting individual and corporate creativity. It worked well in the 19th and 20th centuries, and it will do so into the 21st and 22nd ones too.

Look at some specific opportunities for projects that may stimulate technological and economic growth in the present century.

Proposal A: – **Electric Vehicles**

In the mid-1970's America was plunged into the first energy crisis of the modern era after the Organization of Petroleum Exporting Countries (OPEC) placed an embargo on oil shipments to the United States. In response, the nation rationed gasoline by limiting sales to even or odd days. The federal government also developed research projects to study alternatives to petroleum as a transportation fuel. I spent two summers employed at NASA's Lewis Research Center[5] in Cleveland, Ohio, working on an alternative battery to power postal delivery vans. For the moon rover, NASA already had a very successful battery made from silver and zinc. This rechargeable battery had a much greater electric capacity than

---

[5] Now renamed the NASA John H. Glenn Research Center at Lewis Field.

the common lead acid battery then in general use. More important was the fact that this battery was significantly lighter and cheaper to send into space than the lead-acid battery. This new silver-zinc battery would provide the range needed by postal vans for daily deliveries, was safe, reliable, and rechargeable for at least the expected life of the moon mission. The one problem with this battery was its cost. Each battery pack for a postal van cost about $10,000 in 1976 money, and each van would need two such batteries – one to use while the second one was recharging. This project would not be economically viable even for government use, since one would have to spend $20,000 for the batteries and then spend more to buy the postal van. At that time a full-size Ford station wagon cost only $2,500 brand new. A cheaper battery would have to be found. Our project was to try to make an inexpensive rechargeable nickel-zinc battery reliable enough to survive one thousand cycles or three years.

Others working on the project to develop electric alternative energy sources for transportation had calculated that if a battery could be found that had enough charge to drive 100 miles a day and was light weight enough, cheap, reliable, rechargeable for at least 1000 cycles, and safe, more than 90% of American driving needs could be met with electric vehicles. Battery technology has made great advances over the past four decades. Today batteries having the capability to power even an airplane for a continental flight are within reach.[6] Here is another opportunity for government-industry cooperation.

---

[6] Lithium-Ion batteries have changed daily life making small, portable, reliable batteries available for computers, cellphones, and even Tesla automobiles. These batteries have a specific energy density of about 250 W hr/kg. If a battery could be developed which had a specific energy density of 800 W hr/kg, it could be used to power a Boeing 737 airplane on a 1100 km flight. The Lithium-Air battery now used in

While improved on-board electric storage is being developed is there something that could be done now with existing technology? Yes, there is! Batteries can be recharged in at least two ways. The generally used method is to connect a charger directly to a 110v or 220v electric outlet. This presents a danger in that it is far too easy to contact the hot wire and get a shock or electrocuted. Another way, however, is to use induction. In this method advantage is taken of electrical induction in which the alternating current in the charging paddle induces a charge in the socket on the car enabling the battery to be recharged without the possibility of electrical shock. Some electric cars are already recharged in this way.

Today's electric automobiles have ranges of about 250 miles or more per charge. This ought to be enough to meet most needs of American drivers; but if a safe way could be found to recharge electric vehicles while they are moving, the range could be extended almost infinitely. Place an induction strip in or on the middle of one lane of an interstate highway. Equip an electric car with an induction "pig tail" which could drop down and contact that induction strip. While the car sped along under non-human control in this charging lane, the battery could be recharged. The driver could relax while additional miles were added to the vehicle's range. The limit on a vehicle's range would be the stamina[7] of the driver and not the range of the battery. The recharging could be paid for by using the same payment system now used to pay highway tolls.

---

hearing aids has a theoretical energy density of 3460 W hr/kg. To be useful in transportation this battery must be scaled up and made rechargeable. Opportunities exist. ["Batteries need a boost to fly the friendly skies" by Tien Nguyen and published in Chemical and Engineering News for 28 October 2019 on pages 22-24.]

[7] Or the bladder

At the beginning of the twentieth century America had heavy and light rail systems that enabled Americans to travel on light rail public transportation from Chicago to Boston. As automobiles became more popular and available and as automotive corporations became richer and more powerful, this system of public transportation was bought up and taken out of service by these companies. Efficient public transportation presented a threat to the emerging automotive industry. Public transportation, however, is more economical and environmentally friendly than private automobiles. Encourage the automobile industry and new companies to develop creative solutions for improved public transportation. When my family and I lived in Europe, we did not need to own a car. Public transportation was fast, convenient, and cost-effective. We could get from Halle/Saale in the GDR to West Berlin in two hours using public trams and trains. We did not even need taxis. Why can America not have an effective system of public transportation?   It should be possible for most Americans living in urban areas to get a public bus or streetcar within a few blocks of their homes. If these ran every fifteen to twenty minutes, public transport would be convenient. It can take that long just to find a parking place in today's cities! Rather than owning automobiles, Americans living in cities and suburbs might prefer to use public transport and resort to renting a private automobile only for trips out into the countryside.

Build public transportation systems that are clean, safe, convenient, and efficient.

Encourage Americans to use trains, light rail, and buses for trips of up to three hundred miles or about six hours. Let airplanes fly only for flights of more than three hundred miles. A three-hundred-mile trip on a fast train operating at 100 mph or more will be only about three or four hours. Today, one must arrive two hours early at least at the airport to board a plane. After landing, one must take ground transportation from the airport to the city center. The time spent just getting to and from the airport is equal or greater than the time needed for the entire 300-mile trip by modern efficient public transportation.

Do not use today's inefficient public transportation options in your calculations. Use what could and ought to be rather than what is today in America. We can do better! Do railroad trains have to travel only on two parallel steel rails? Is there some other, perhaps faster and safer way? Can passengers travel in their automobiles that can be loaded and unloaded while the train is in motion? Let's be imaginative and creative again!

How can such changes be encouraged by a forward-thinking government? One way is to discourage the use of private cars for daily commutes into cities by taking some actions now.

1. Make parking fees subject to a tax and use this revenue to help pay for improved public transportation.
2. Add a fuel tax on carbon-based fuels. Charge a carbon fuel tax of perhaps 10% and increase this each year. Use this revenue to help pay for improved public transportation.
3. Refuse to fund or approve any highway projects for roadways that already have three lanes each way until an improved public transportation plan is in place and implemented.
4. Subsidize parking garages outside of cities at public transportation hubs.

5. Support research and development in public-private projects that find ways to reduce most commutes to twenty minutes or less each way.

6. Insist that no building permits for housing or building projects are to be issued until after water, sewer, electricity, high-speed internet, and public transportation infrastructure projects are implemented and in place. Insist, as a goal, that all plans for new industrial, business, and residential building keep commutes to under twenty minutes.

Proposal C: – Revisit the AC/DC Debate.

When electricity was being developed at the end of the nineteenth century, there was a debate between Thomas Edison and Nikola Tesla. This is referred to as the "Battle of the Currents."[8] Edison advocated for the use of DC current because of its relative safety, while Tesla favored AC current because it could easily be transformed up and down using transformers and because there was much less loss when electricity was transmitted over distances at high voltages. In fact, both currents had advantages and disadvantages. High voltage AC could be quite dangerous unless rigid safety procedures were followed. [9] During the height of this battle of the currents, Edison and others opposed to high voltage AC demonstrated its dangers by electrocuting animals and criminals using George Westinghouse's high voltage AC.

There were two decisive events that helped select AC current as the type that would be used in the United States.

---

[8] Information from websites: https://www.energy.gov/articles/war-currents-ac-vs-dc-power and https://www.energy.gov/edison-vs-tesla.
[9] Residents of California know all too well the dangers of wildfires presented by high voltage transmission lines.

The 1893 Chicago World's Fair[10] solicited bids to electrify the exposition. Edison and his General Electric Company made a bid to use DC current, while George Westinghouse made a lower bid to electrify the fair using Tesla's AC current. The lower bid won the contract. The fair amazed those who attended and helped spread electrification to the nation.

The second decisive event in the Battle of the Currents was the decision to award the contract to generate electricity at Niagara Falls to Westinghouse using AC current in 1893. By 1896, the city of Buffalo, NY, was electrified using the AC current from the Niagara Falls Electric Generating Plant. At this point, Edison gave up on DC current and switched to AC current for the further electrification of New York City.

It is only because of rigid safety standards that the AC system in use now is safe enough to use. Today, however, it is possible to conveniently generate electricity with solar panels at the location of use. Now it is possible to convert DC current to high voltages with modern technology. China, in fact, has several high voltage DC transmission lines (HVDC). Does the U.S. have any? Perhaps it is time to revisit the AC/DC debate. Can DC electric current be generated economically and reliably near the locus of use in homes and industries? Does the nation really need high voltage AC transmission lines? Would it be more economical, safer, and environmentally friendly to use locally produced DC current? Could electric motors be smaller, cheaper, and more reliable using DC current? Could electrical appliances be made to run more efficiently, safely, and reliably on 12, 24, 48, or other low voltage DC? Let us revisit that question and decide which is more appropriate for today's technology and needs.

---

[10] This was officially called the World's Columbian Exposition.

The destruction of the electrical grid in Puerto Rico from Hurricane Maria in September 2017 could have been an ideal opportunity to give a practical demonstration of options available and help our nation decide which electrical system would be better in today's world. The government did nothing to take advantage of this opportunity. It may just have been an opportunity lost. With nature raging, I am confident that we shall have other opportunities to have practical demonstrations of which electrical system is better.

In the mid-1970's when NASA was researching electric automobiles at the Cleveland center, the electric car being tested used DC motors not AC alternators.

Proposal D: – Make Products Durable.

If products were made to last or to be recycled in ways that do not alter the environment, less of the earth's resources would be consumed and disposal problems would be reduced. Pollution would be reduced. This could be facilitated by several government actions.

Mandate that every product made and sold must last a decade or be recyclable unless designed to be consumed immediately. Every manufacturer must put a permanent identification mark on each product giving the company of manufacture and the year of production. If the product fails before the mandated decade, the manufacturer is responsible for taking it back and either repairing it or recycling it. If recycled or placed in a landfill, it must decompose naturally so as not to alter the environment. Instead of buying twenty-five automobiles over a lifetime, each person might only buy six or fewer.

This rule would apply to single-use plastic bags as well as durable goods such as appliances. Manufacturers need to discover ways to make products decompose quickly and safely in the environment leaving no harmful or long-lasting residue. The final decomposition product must be compatible with a clean environment. Microbes and ultraviolet light may be helpful. Plastic grocery bags must cease to be blown by the wind onto barbwire fences and into bushes and trees. Waste plastics must stop coating the oceans. Chemists, biologists, physicists, and microbiologists can all make contributions in this effort to conserve the environment. Everyone must pitch in to preserve a viable environment.

Generally, if you make it, you are going to be responsible for taking it back. Recycling should become part of the purchase price of each product. Let us begin to think long term. Think about the effect our actions are going to have on two or three generations in the future.

Proposal E: – Discover the Ocean Depths.

Mankind has spent time, money, and considerable effort to explore the moon, planets, and outer space; but it has done little to learn what is at the bottom of the oceans and in the sea. Let us spend some time and effort to explore our own backyard. What resources might be found there? We know that large deposits of manganese nodules exist on the ocean floor. Are there similar deposits of rare earths down there? What energy sources can we discover by more fully understanding the physical chemistry of ocean vents? Let us get wet and get busy.

10. **Gerrymandering Election Districts**

Politicians have used all kinds of tricks and rouses to gain an unfair advantage over other viewpoints, beliefs, and opponents. One of the most common and heinous is the practice of gerrymandering election districts in such ways as to give themselves an advantage. This is unfair, unwise, and undemocratic. Voters should be grouped not by race, religion, ethnic origin, political party preferences, or any other irrelevant criteria. They should be grouped with their neighbors with whom they share a common geography, agricultural and economic interests, environmental concerns, and transportation, education, and infrastructure needs.

Fortunately, in America this has already been done historically when political subdivisions were initially created. Advantage should be taken of this when establishing electoral districts for both federal and state elections. By following a few simple rules, electoral districts could be much fairer for all.

The following are some suggested rules for establishing electoral districts in state and federal elections:

1. The populations of all districts created must be as equal as possible within a prescribed variation.

2. All districts must be contiguous and compact. As much as possible, each electoral district should share similar geographical, social, and economic features such as river valleys, mountain ranges, climate, and agricultural and economic bases.

3. No existing political subdivision such as a county, town, or city may be subdivided unless there is absolutely no other way to equalize the populations of each district. As far as possible, political subdivision boundaries must be respected when establishing election districts. Political subdivisions may not be subdivided unless prior approval is obtained from the courts. The courts should demand proof that there is no other alternative to equalize the number of voters in each district. It should be very rare that an existing political subdivision be divided more than once.

4. Keep it as simple and fair as possible.

11. **Three DARPA Proposals**
[Details to be submitted to DARPA upon request]

Proposal A: – **Detonation at a Distance.**

This proposal suggests research funding that would enable the safe detonation of explosives at a distance (DAAD). If successful, this proposal would enable the rapid, safe, and economical removal of land mines; the premature and harmless detonation of IED's; the premature and safe detonation of all suicide bombs in explosion rooms as luggage, cargo, and passengers pass through checkpoints. Further, since all nuclear weapons use carefully timed explosive charges to initiate the atomic detonation, such weapons would be rendered hazardous to have, since they could be detonated while in storage or en route to targets. The basics of conventional warfare would be dramatically changed since DAAD could detonate any and all explosives used in rifles, tanks, warships, or airplanes. Since the same chemical principles underlying DAAD are used in rocket fuels, missiles also would not be safe to store with fuel.

DETAILS OF DAAD: ***REDACTED***

Proposal B: – **The Starlings Project**

Recall how a simple bird strike caused a passenger airplane to crash land in the Hudson River. This project will have two modes of operation. One will prevent an aircraft from taking off and the other will bring it down

once airborne. Recall also how a flock of starlings fly in unison in murmuration.
 DETAILS of Project Starling: **REDACTED**

Proposal C: – **The Squid Project**
A weapon would be developed that would stop ship movement and navigation on and under the seas.
DETAILS of the Squid Project: **REDACTED**

12. United Nations Security Council Membership and Responsibilities

One reason the League of Nations failed to prevent wars before World War II was that it proved to be unable to prevent aggression such as Italy's invasion of Ethiopia in the 1930's under Mussolini. The United Nations is following the same path to failure. It is now time to revise the U.N. Charter to avoid the same failure to maintain peace.

The U.N. Security Council membership should be revised to make it an effective organ for world peace. Three modifications are needed.

First, all members of the Security Council both temporary and permanent must contribute personnel and equipment to an U. N. International Police Force (IPF). This force will be used to immediately deploy when events in any nation create problems and costs for another.

When events in one nation spill over into another forcing the neighbor to expend funds, this internal problem becomes an international one and an issue for the U.N. International Police Force. The International Police Force would intervene in a country when domestic chaos spills over into its neighbors. When gangs, drugs, criminal activity, economic or political changes cause law abiding citizens to seek asylum in another country, this International Police Force could intervene to help the local government restore order. Examples here include civil war in Syria and economic and environmental devastation in Honduras, Guatemala, and El Salvador. These all created refugees.

A second change would be to use this International Police Force to intervene when one nation invades another. All changes in borders must be orderly and only by ballot in all countries involved. A recent example would be Russia's forced annexation of the Crimea and her incursion into the Donbas region of eastern Ukraine.

A problem occurs, however, when one of the member nations of the Security Council itself is a law and peace breaker. In this case, the perpetrating nation must be stripped of its membership on the U.N. Security Council. If it is a temporary member, it is simply replaced by the General Assembly. If it one of the five permanent members, its membership on the Security Council is suspended until the borders are restored to the way they were before any invasion or annexation. Example: Russian invasion of Ukraine and its annexation of the Crimea.

A third change would be to use the International Police Force to intervene in any nation that developed and possessed weapons of mass destruction including biological, chemical, and nuclear. Examples include North Korea (PRK), Iran, Pakistan, India, and Israel. Slowly but surely the U.N. should work toward the total elimination of such weapons of mass destruction. Eventually all nations must surrender such weapons to the U.N. International Police Force.

13. **National Debt Reduction Plan for the United States**

Those who make obscenely large incomes in America are the very ones who have benefitted the most from America's investments in its infrastructure, defense, etc. These are the ones who should bear the burden of making major contributions to paying down the nation's debt. The same should apply to state debts. The general population should not be expected to bear the entire burden.

For the sake of a simplified argument, assume that the population of the United States is about 330 million. From this there may be about 100 million taxpayers. If 1% of these taxpayers are the obscenely rich, then there will be about 1 million such taxpayers who would be obligated to pay down this debt.

To determine who is in this category, consider the salary table given in topic 7. The first line includes all taxpayers who make a minimum wage of $10/hour for a total of 8 hours per day, 5 days a week, 52 weeks a year for a total of 2080 hours per year. This amounts to about $20,800 per year. The other lines show annual salaries for multiples of this basic minimum wage that are earned in shorter periods of time.

Those who make a truly obscenely high income should be grouped together and they should pay an additional tax based on the size of the national debt. This group should be expected to pay down or pay off the debt in a fixed number of years. Consider the example above.

Assume that the very wealthy 1% fall into this obscene income bracket. That means that there should be about one million such taxpayers able to pay down the nation's debt.   After C_2O Trump and his Republicans, the nation's debt now has risen to 1 trillion dollars. If the group of high earners is given 25 years to pay off the debt, each one of them will only have to contribute an average of an additional $40,000 per year. They can afford that much. That is not even the cost of one luxury automobile! This is fair, since this group is the one that took advantage of the investments made in infrastructure, education, defense, environment, etc. that make it possible for them to accrue such wealth.

Sample Calculation Details:

The nation's debt after Trump's Republican additions now stands at about one trillion dollars, ($1.0x10^{12}$). Divide this total debt by the number of obscenely high-income taxpayers and divide it again by the number of years over which the debt is to be retired.

$$\$(1.0 \times 10^{12}) \div (1.0 \times 10^{6}) \div 25yr = \$40,000 \text{ per year}$$
per high income taxpayer

Such an amount is manageable. The rest of the population will help pay the interest on the debt, but the principal will be paid by the wealthiest one percent.

To further help the national economy, take the following actions to rid the swamp of the parasitic alligators:

1. No individual, organization, or political party may accept government funds from anyone or any

agency unless these have been paid for in advance. Specifically, individuals may continue to receive Social Security, Medicare, and retirement benefits from the government treasury because these benefits were ostensibly paid for in advance by the participants. These may have become poorly structured and badly funded programs as a result of politicians attempting to purchase votes using the public treasury, but they still are programs that return money to those who made investments in these programs in good faith.

2. Let this nation return to politicians who serve the people and the nation rather than themselves and their friends. No person may be re-elected to any office more than once. Get in, get the job done, and get out letting someone else have a chance to contribute. Politics should be a service to the nation. It must never again become a job or a career. A person may be re-elected to an office held more than two terms only after being out of that office at least as long as he or she was in that office. No politicians may receive a retirement for that service. Elected office should be an opportunity to serve others not a way to get rich.

14. **Politics in the Electronic Age**

There may be an advantage in dividing the federal legislative branch into ten geographical regions and joining these regions electronically. It is possible today to meet and conduct business at a distance using modern electronic media. Skype and other programs make this possible. Businesses, corporations, medical professions, military, governmental agencies, and educational institutions already do this successfully. Doing so in Congress will increase efficiency in government and bring the members of the House and Senate closer to the citizens they represent.

Let the members of Congress meet regularly together in person in Washington, D.C., at least once each session. Let them meet from early January for several weeks to be sworn in, establish the rules for each house, organize committees, elect chairmen, and conduct other necessary organizational business. After Inauguration Day they will be able to disperse into their respective regional districts and conduct business electronically from there. After Inauguration Day, the members of Congress will meet in person only in their respective regions. They will meet regularly together as a body connected electronically from these regions coming together physically in Washington, D.C., only when necessary and when agreed upon. These physical joint meetings in the Capitol might be necessary only in extraordinary situations such as the need to approve a final budget on time, confirm Supreme Court justices, or conduct impeachment hearings.

Meeting electronically by regions will expedite proceedings, reduce travel costs, reduce office costs, and bring the members of Congress closer to the citizens they represent. It will increase the number of citizens able to contact their representatives. It will enable members of Congress to conduct and conclude more of the nation's business in a timely manner. Less travel time and costs will be required. It will make life more difficult and more costly for lobbyists.

Let the members of each region of Congress meet regularly in person at one or more mutually agreed upon locations within each of the ten geographical regions. Each region will have the same number of senators but a varying number of representatives. The regional meeting sites may be changed periodically or may rotate regularly. It could even move among the five state capitols in each region. When meeting in these regions, committees and chambers will be connected electronically with members in other regions. Both houses of Congress will still conduct business as usual but do so joined electronically.

Because the regions will be contiguous and have similar geographical and economic concerns, the members of Congress will more efficiently understand and serve the needs of their citizens.

The political regions must be mutually agreed upon. The number of Senators in each political region will always be ten. The number of Representatives for each political region will vary from about six to about seventy-four. It may be better, however, to preserve regional similarities and interests rather than to have equal numbers. After all, the entire Congress as a whole will still meet electronically to conduct business as is now the case.

A possible initial arrangement of political regions might be similar to the groupings in the following table:

Region	States	Senators	Representatives
I	ME, NH, MA, RI, CT	10	20
II	VT, NY, NJ, PA, OH	10	74
III	MD, DE,VA,WV, NC	10	36
IV	SC, GA, FL, AL, MS	10	59
V	MI, IN, IL, KY, TN	10	56
VI	MN, WI, IA, MO, AR	10	32
VII	LA, TX, OK, KS, NB	10	54
VIII	ND, SD, MT, WY, ID	10	6
IX	AZ, NM, NV, UT, CO	10	27
X	WA, OR, CA, AK, HI	10	71

15. Reform American Politics–Service not Careers

Not long after the beginning of the American Experiment in democracy in the early years of the nineteenth century, professional politicians appeared. These were individuals who viewed and treated election to an office to be a career opportunity rather than a chance to serve the nation. They began to serve themselves or their party rather than a chance to serve others. It progressively got worse as the decades passed. Soon they were voting themselves special privileges, e.g., salaries way above actual expenses and unbelievably generous healthcare and retirement packages not available to the average citizen. Yes, they worked hard to milk the system!

To begin a reformation in politics, it is necessary to remove the incentives making it a career. No one should be re-elected to the same office more than once until they have been out of that office for as long as they have continuously been in an office. Get elected, get to work, make your contribution, get the job done, and get out of the way making room for the next American.

Get the money out of politics. The Supreme Court was unwise to open the money floodgates for politics. Allow every candidate to use no more than a fixed amount of money, e.g., 10 dollars for each vote cast in the last general election in each district. This money will come from a general, public fund to pay for elections. No other money may be spent by or for any candidate. Rich and poor candidates will be equal.

When the courts ruled that spending limitations in elections were a violation of the Constitutional guarantee for free speech, they considered only part of the question and ruled in favor of special interests. I am not rich; I have little or no money to give to politicians or their political parties. Consequently, the Supreme Court stole my right to "free" speech. They made it so that only money talks, and I and many other citizens are condemned to silence. We can only keep silent, for we do not have the amount of money required to speak out. Free speech ceases to be free when it is for sale. The Supreme Court should have looked around and asked what about the rest of us who are not rich enough to be able to afford "free" speech.

16. **Apply a Thirty-Day Rule Twice**

America's success is due largely to the Constitution which requires that decisions be made by three, equal, independent branches of government and not by one branch and certainly never by one individual. That irrevocable decision was made when King George III was removed from American affairs in 1776. The country has gotten into difficult situations only when that rule was violated. World War II was the last time that the United States won a war. It was also the last time that the Congress declared war. All the war-like actions since 1945 were undeclared by Congress. At least one branch of the government failed. Specifically, Congress failed to discharge its Constitutional duty. Members of Congress were allowed to abdicate their responsibilities. The politicians managed to avoid blame for the resulting events, costs, and sacrifices. And, what happened? We lost.

The "Police Action in Korea" was not a declared war. There was no rationing. The entire nation was not mobilized. Only a few, mainly veterans, went to war. We did not win. The Vietnam conflict was also not a war. It was fought mainly by draftees. Congress again failed to act. The Gulf of Tonkin Resolution was not a declaration of war, yet a treasury was depleted, and an entire generation of Americans suffered. For what? Congress should have fulfilled its duty and discovered that this may have been merely a poorly disguised effort to help France out of a difficult situation in the final remnants of French Indochina and to prop up a corrupt puppet government in South Vietnam. Could this action by JFK really have been a response to satisfy a persistent request from his wife, Jackie, who loved France and all things French? The entire theory of falling dominoes was fallacious, made-up. What fell after our defeat? We now purchase our clothes, electric fans, fish, shoes, and shrimp from Vietnam. Congress in its deliberations should have discovered if war was justified. Was it worth it? We lost and left. We lost an entire generation of our young people, and we turned our backs on them when they returned. It was not their fault. The self-serving members of Congress are to be blamed for their failure to scrutinize the need for such military action. If it were justified, war should have been declared by Congress before the first American soldier was sent overseas. The entire nation should have become involved. There was no rationing. There were no increased war taxes or even war bonds. What were the members of Congress thinking? Why did we ever let them get away with such a dereliction of duty?

Such Congressional failures continue to the present day. The Second Iraq War was also undeclared. Congress again failed to scrutinize the justifications for such action. They failed to uncover that the intelligence about Iraqi chemical weapons of mass destruction was wrong. Could it have been that George Bush and his administration were far too willing to accept partial, flawed intelligence because he wanted to get back at Saddam Hussein trying to have his father assassinated while on a victory visit to Kuwait after the first Gulf War? What did Congress' failure to fulfill its responsibilities cost the nation? What is it still costing us?

No. Never Again! Before Americans are sent overseas into a conflict, Congress must declare the nation to be at war after a very careful debate.   When war is declared, the entire nation must become involved personally. To ensure that this happens, apply a thirty-day rule: On the thirty-first day that American service men and women are involved in an armed conflict overseas, everyone in the country will pay a 10% surcharge in taxes and withholdings. After an additional ninety days if these additional funds are insufficient to pay for the war, the taxes go up again and so on.   The members of Congress will have to continuously justify to themselves and the American people that this action and these sacrifices are necessary. The politicians must face consequences.   Members of Congress must never again be allowed to evade responsibility and fail to discharge their responsibilities.

The Thirty-Day Rule should be applied in a second case also. There are and will be times when immediate action is necessary before Congress has an opportunity to act. The President, when we have one, should be able to issue Executive Orders to address these immediate needs. Storms come, earthquakes happen, and forests burn. The President must act quickly to address the immediate needs. He must also present a proposal to Congress for any long-term solutions. It is Congress that must act on his request. The President must never again be able to act as a dictator and rule in the absence of Congressional action. Make any and all Presidential Executive orders effective for no more than thirty days, or less if Congress acts. The President must justify his action as necessary and persuade Congress to act. No Presidential Executive Order may be extended beyond thirty-days nor may it be reissued. It is Congress that must act! By being able to meet and act electronically, Congress should be able to do so within the allowed time. The President, if he truly is a leader, will be able to persuade Congress and the nation to do so.

17. **Internet and Postal Reform**

The internet, which was made possible by advances in technology spurred on by the race to the moon, has greatly altered the way humans interact and communicate. Communication has become faster and more convenient; but perhaps there should be some limitations because it has become invasive. Instead of being a tool to improve efficiency, it has been allowed to become our new master. We are in danger of becoming a slave to an electronic device. In regular, surface mail (aka snail mail), there is a return address. The sender should be known and publicly available even though the contents of letters and electronic messages remain private, available only to the recipient. There should also be a cost in causing others to spend time reading and responding to a sender's message. There should be a cost to using this service. Regular mail requires a delivery address, return address, and postage stamp. Electronic messages should be treated similarly.

As with regular mail, the recipient should be able to determine whether a letter or message should be opened and read or merely discarded as worthless. So very much of my mail is junk. I do not waste time even opening it. I simply throw it into or send it to the trash saving both my time and money. With electronic mail, I do not waste time reading about so-and-so's cat's daily antics.

Let the internet run through the U.S. Postal Service and every message, posting, tweet, advertisement, etc. would have to have an address, return address, and postage paid. Impose a minimal fee of perhaps one mil, $0.001, per such message. In that way the sender of every message would be known.   People will think before sending frivolous and time-wasting messages.   The internet could become even more convenient and useful. The U.S. Postal Service may again make money for the federal treasury.   Any person or company or country planning to use the American internet would have to establish an account with the U.S. Postal Service. The fees would be withdrawn from this account as messages, postings, tweets, etc. were sent.

A ten-dollar account would pay for 10,000 postings at a mil each.   Such is enough to last a long time except for those who for selfish or nefarious reasons want to waste recipients' time or foment discord and civil disorder. Such a fee might reduce messages sent merely to separate the recipient from his or her money by trying to sell them something they neither need nor want.

Since the sender of every message and posting would be known, anyone sending, posting, or forwarding dangerous or terrorist posts or messages could be reported by recipients to postal inspectors. If found to be dangerous, the sender's account could be closed and access to the internet be denied.

All messages originating from out of the country could readily be identified and if being used to influence public opinion and American elections could likewise be removed from the internet.   The International Postal Union could be expanded to cover international electronic messages.

Just as with regular surface mail, such a payment system must not be used to limit free inquiry or speech but would prevent senders of electronic mail from "shouting fire in a crowded theater."

18. **Enforce the Constitutional Mandate Prohibiting a President from Financially Benefitting from his Position. Enforce the emoluments clause.**

The Constitution mandates that the President shall not financially benefit from his office. He especially is forbidden from accepting money or favors from foreigners and foreign governments.

The present and any future President or C_2O will have to return to the U.S. Treasury any and all funds with interest that he, his family, or his business interests received while he was in office unless those funds were received for services rendered after a fair, open, and competitive bidding process as is required by law. All gifts and funds received from foreign citizens or governments must be turned over to the U.S. Treasury. The President and government officials are entitled to their salaries and that is enough.

To be certain that nothing is overlooked, the tax returns of government officials, including the President, must be made public both before and after taking office.

19. **Every Government is Responsible for Its Citizens and the Regulation of Migration**

Every citizen owes allegiance to his own country, and likewise every country has a responsibility for each one of its citizens. When a citizen of one country travels into another country, that responsibility does not end. If the new host country grants entry or a visa to the citizen of another country, then the host country accepts temporary responsibility for both the physical and fiscal wellbeing of the guest. If a citizen of one country enters another without such an invitation or permit, then the country of citizenship still retains fiscal responsibility for its citizens. The country of citizenship must reimburse the host country for all expenses incurred by its citizens while in another country uninvited. U.S. states being forced to support uninvited guests may bill the federal government for health, education, welfare, etc. costs they incur. The federal government will reimburse the states and bill and collect the money from the country of citizenship for each uninvited guest.

Families will no longer be separated at the American border and migrants will not be denied entry. Neither the states nor the federal government will have to bear the costs of supporting uninvited guests. The governments of uninvited guests may request the return of their citizens after they receive bills for services rendered. While this process is going on, questions of asylum may be addressed in the courts. Uninvited guests may be granted entry visas or be required to return to the countries of their citizenship.

Failure to pay the bills presented by the host country becomes an admission of being a failed state. Any failed state that incurs a large debt becomes an issue for the United Nations to consider. No nation may force its problems on another.

Examples abound -- Somalia, the Balkans, Syria, Central America, etc. To restore world peace and order, the U.N. may recommend a forced change in government or even a change in boundaries. No country may permit its troubles to spill over to another. No country may oppress or persecute a minority for racial, ethnic, or religious reasons.

20. **Replace Marriage with an Intent to Propagate (ITP)**

This proposal is **NOT** to be taken seriously. It is put forward merely to force readers to think about the issues fairly. NB: This is **NOT** to be done! The way to correct a wrong is seldom successful by creating another wrong.

When a woman becomes pregnant, her life changes irreversibly, forever. What if society could arrange for the life of the male to also have a life-altering change? Would people re-think their current views on sex, abortion, and women's rights?

Let society take advantage of advances made in science since the Medieval Period. Require that every child born or naturalized in the U.S. have their DNA determined. Do the same for every mother and father. No man or woman shall ever again be able to claim that he or she is not the real parent of a child. Every child will know for sure who their biological mother and father are. In the future, this knowledge will become even more important in determining effective medical care. This also means that no one may escape paying the costs of bringing a child into the world. Even sperm and egg donors cannot escape or transfer their financial responsibilities to someone else, onto the public treasury, or onto a company or organization. If it is your sperm or egg that was used to create a child, that child becomes your responsibility forever or at least until they reach the age of maturity, e.g., 18 or 21.

So far, so good. Now the controversial part of this fictitious proposal.

Every man or woman who agrees to engage in sexual intercourse or to have their egg or sperm used to do so, must first execute an Intent-To-Propagate (ITP) document. It must be signed, notarized, and recorded in a local courthouse. This eliminates any questions that may arise as to whether sexual intercourse was consensual.

If intercourse or egg/sperm donation happens without such an ITP document being on record, the woman must carry the fetus to term, and the man must be irreversibly castrated. The male must experience a life-altering event as does the female. Now that there is some equality of consequences, you may sit down and decide on sex, abortion, and women's rights.

Any couple that has a religious or civil marriage service, has it notarized and recorded will be assumed to have executed an ITP.

Any individual or couple who decides no longer to propagate may simply execute a document declaring so. If this is signed, notarized, and recorded and if a ninety-day waiting period has occurred, individuals are free to enter a new ITP. The ninety-day waiting period is to make sure that no pregnancy resulted from the original ITP.

Any individual, man or woman, who wishes to execute an ITP with someone else while still having a valid ITP may do so after posting a bond with the state of residence. This bond must be equal to the cost of raising a child to the age of maturity. This bond will be returned if the additional ITP is rescinded and the ninety-day waiting period has expired without a pregnancy. It will also be returned when all children reach maturity. The state will keep the interest on earned on the bond to cover expenses for the program. If the child is adopted, the adopted parents will be able to use the funds in the bond to pay expenses for the child.

SCIENTIFIC HYPOTHESES APPLIED TO POLITICS
By
Patrick Barber, Ph.D.

Science has made great strides forward in understanding and living more in harmony with nature since the adoption of the scientific method in the seventeenth century. All scientific hypotheses begin with a public presentation of the basic hypothesis, which is not an accusation. It is a "what if" statement put forward so that others may also help find facts (data) to test the hypothesis. The purpose of the hypothesis is to stimulate subsequent investigations. The entire field advances when the rules are followed. The rules are simple but important.

Before any hypothesis is advanced publicly, there must be at least some physical evidence supporting it. There must be some evidence, some data, suggesting that the proposed hypothesis might be valid. There is in addition, however, one cardinal rule that must never ever be violated. This rule forbids anyone from falling in love with a hypothesis. One may not accept only data supporting a proposed hypothesis while selectively rejecting data refuting it. All data must be treated and evaluated fairly. If these rules are followed, science advances, pushing back the curtain of ignorance.

The use of hypotheses has generally been limited to science. Recently, however, some people have begun to use them in the field of politics. Those who do attempt this must follow the basic rules that have been used so successfully in science. What follows is an explanation of why one of these recent attempts to apply hypotheses to politics was wrong. This is followed by an illustration of applying hypotheses to politics following the basic rules.

Those who proposed the "Birther Hypothesis" provide a good example of violating both principles stated above.   The hypothesis under review proposed that Barack Obama was ineligible to be President of the U.S. because he had not been born in the United States. This would have been an acceptable hypothesis when first proposed if there had been any evidence supporting it. The mere fact that Barack Obama's father had been a Kenyan citizen says nothing about the physical location of his child's birth or the child's citizenship. It would have been better if the proponents could find data indicating that Barack's mother was physically out of the United States at the time of his birth, but no such data was advanced when the hypothesis was first proposed. It is true that the hypothesis stimulated further gathering of facts. Those who continued to support the "Birther Hypothesis" after the State of Hawaii verified that Mr. Obama did indeed have a valid birth certificate also violated the cardinal rule. That piece of evidence should have immediately terminated the "Birther Hypothesis. They were guilty of selectively excluding concrete data refuting the hypothesis while they continued in vain to find some to support it.

Since this group began applying hypotheses to politics, let me continue; but let me avoid the two errors made by those proposing the "Birther hypothesis." Let me begin with an initial proposition: Vladimir Putin, President of Russia, is a very smart man [The Hypothesis].

As with all hypotheses, there must be some basic physical evidence to support it at the time of presentation. Those who supported the "Birther Hypothesis" had nothing more than speculation. In the hypothesis that I am proposing, there is some actual data supporting it. Look at some facts about Putin's life. Putin was born in Leningrad, USSR, which has since been renamed Saint Petersburg, Russia, on 7 October 1952. He studied law at Leningrad State University and after graduation joined the Soviet Committee on State Security, KGB, one of the world's best intelligence agencies. They did not hire dummies. While he worked in the KGB, he served for years in Dresden, East Germany, where his attention was focused on defeating the U.S. NATO, and the West. After the Soviet Union collapsed in 1990-1991, he retired from the KGB with the rank of Lieutenant Colonel. Dummies generally do not get promoted. He returned to his hometown of Saint Petersburg and became an administrator at his alma mater and active in city politics. One of his academic mentors at the university was Anatoly Sobchak, who had been active in the Perestroika movement and was active in city politics. In Saint Petersburg under Sobchak, Putin earned a reputation as someone who could get things done. He rose quickly becoming first deputy mayor. In 1996 he moved to Moscow and continued his rapid rise. President Boris Yeltsin made him director of the Federal Security Service (FSB), which was the successor to the Soviet KGB. One does not rise so quickly and so high and not be a very smart individual. Conclusion: All evidence gathered so far supports the hypothesis that Putin is very smart, talented, and hard working.[11], [12], [13], [14]

In addition to being smart, Putin seems to be ruthless and determined to have his way. He may have ordered, merely suggested, or turned a blind eye to the detention and murder of his opponents. He ordered or supported the Russian invasion and takeover of the Crimea. There may be evidence suggesting that he may be as mean as Ivan the Terrible. There seems to be evidence also suggesting that he might have to be ranked with Peter the Great and Catherine the Great.

It should be noted that all of Putin's early education, career, and training were in trying to find ways to destroy and defeat the United States, NATO, and Western Europe. [Corollary #1] Could it be that he is still trying to disrupt and defeat the West? We do not know.

---

[11] Vladimir Putin, Principal Website in English:
eng.putin.kremlin.ru>bio
[12] Vladimir Putin, Biography by Biography.com Editors:
https://www.biography.com/political-figure/vladimir-putin
[13] Vladimir Putin, Wikipedia:
https://en.wikipedia.org>wiki>Vladimir_Putin
[14] Vladimir Putin published by Encyclopedia Britannica, Inc.:
https://britannica.com/biography/Vladimir-Putin

Perhaps someone else can uncover evidence to support or refute this corollary to the basic hypothesis that he is smart. There is some initial data supporting this corollary. In his early career that is exactly what he was trained to do.

On 10 October 2019, the BBC posted on-line a report of an interview with Egon Krenz, who had been the last Minister-President of the German Democratic Republic, GDR. He reported the night that the Berlin Wall fell in 1989 was "the worst night of my life." Like Putin, Egon Krenz, who was born in 1937, rose rapidly. He replaced Erich Honecker as head of the East German government soon after that nation celebrated its 40th anniversary. In the BBC interview Mr. Krenz insisted, "The Cold War never ended" instead it is "being fought now with different methods." If Mr. Krenz is correct, Putin could be the architect of those different methods. Corollary #1 to the hypothesis may have some support, so it too may be advanced.

From Putin's training and experience he must surely have concluded that America cannot be defeated by an external enemy. It must be taken down from within. The very fabric of American democracy must be shredded. He had years to think about how to establish a fifth column inside the U.S. and finally bring Russia's arch enemy down.

If he could find, cultivate, and support someone who could be manipulated, even unknowingly, to do his bidding, Putin's plan just might succeed. He would have to find someone who was not very well educated, who did not read much, who was ignorant of history, who was not able to think critically, and who was above all else vain and self-centered. [Corollary #2] Into his lap in 2013 fell Donald Trump, who came to Moscow to put on a beauty pageant. Mr. Trump was ready-made to be Putin's man inside Washington. Mr. Trump had everything that Putin needed for the job of tearing down America from the inside. He was not well educated. Although he claimed to have earned college degrees, he has never released his transcripts. Unverified reports claim that he seldom attended classes, never took notes or read textbooks, and was satisfied to merely pass. He claims to be rich but has declared bankruptcy repeatedly and has refused to release his tax returns. By his own public admission, he easily falls into sexual temptations and is therefore subject to blackmail. He knows little history even in the fields he claims to know the best --- business and economics. He imposed tariffs on the American people even though the world learned decades before that these were not wise or effective. After all, it was the Smoot-Hawley Tariffs of 1930 that exacerbated the Great Depression and helped deny Herbert Hoover a second term as President.

Do some of Mr. Trump's words, tweets, and actions also support Corollary #2? Review what has transpired since January 2017. Trump met in private with Putin in Helsinki. Was this a personal business meeting or something more? We do not know; he confiscated and hid the translator's notes. After firing FBI Director Comey, he met with Russian diplomats and news media in the Oval Office but excluded American media. His words and tweets have repeatedly worked to weaken and dismantle

NATO. In Syria he undid the work and sacrifices of many Americans and Kurds to Russia's benefit. His tweets, words, and actions have split Turkey from the NATO alliance. Russia wins again! With his tariff taxes on Americans, he has singlehandedly disrupted decades of building American trading partnerships and relationships. He has through neglect and bad personnel decisions decimated and demoralized the U.S. State Department and the USAID program that helped protect the nation and further its security and business opportunities. He has abandoned the rest of the world of business leaving it to the Chinese and Russians to walk in and pick up the pieces. It has taken thirty years for U.S. Agriculture to develop markets in China and Asia. With a few pen strokes Mr. Trump destroyed all this work. He surrendered to Turkey, Russia, and Syria the Kurdish people who are the principal American allies working to defeat ISIS. ISIS will rise again. Putin wins again in Syria, Iran, and Iraq. Putin wins everywhere. All Trump's actions, words, and tweets are to the advantage of Putin, Russia, China, and PRK. America's friends, allies, and trading partners are in a quandary and turmoil. Putin and other officials in Moscow must be smiling broadly. Could all this be support for Corollary #2? Could Trump be Putin's man in Washington, and could he be so unknowingly?

Yes, Putin may have found his man in Washington. If so, he needed a handler to help control him. [Potential Corollary #3] As a possible further corollary, Mr. Trump's third wife, Melania, would be perfect for the job. No one would suspect even though she was born and raised under

Communism in Yugoslavia. Who eavesdrops on conversations between a husband and his wife? Putin may even have met her on a visit to Slovenia before she married Trump. Was Melania's father, Viktor Knavs, an official in the communist government in Slovenia? Facts are needed to support or refute this corollary. At this point it is important to note that to formally present Corollary #3 would be to repeat the error made by those who supported the "Birther Hypothesis." In order to be presented publicly, a hypothesis or a corollary must have some physical evidence that gives it initial credence. This potential Corollary #3 fails to muster even the minimum factual data needed to enable it to be presented. Pure speculation will not do. Potential Corollary #3 will not be presented until some factual data exist to support it.

Now that the hypothesis and its two corollaries have been presented, it remains to broaden the search and to gather data supporting or refuting them. Hopefully an impeachment trial will enable facts to be uncovered. If the hypothesis and its two corollaries are found to be valid, one may have to conclude that in America today there are Real American Republicans and there are Russian Republicans.

Postscript

In retrospect it appears as if the words and actions of Mr. Khizr Kahn at the Democratic National Convention in July 2016 were prophetic. He generously offered to give Mr. Trump his copy of the U.S. Constitution. If Mr. Trump had accepted that offer, the nation would be far better off today. If Mr. Trump had read (if he can read) the Constitution, he personally would be better off. Can Mr. Trump pass a high school civics course? Does he know and understand the U.S. Constitution?